J

ELIZABETH RING

ASSISTANCE DOGS

IN SPECIAL SERVICE

GOOD DOGS!
THE MILLBROOK PRESS ▪ BROOKFIELD, CONNECTICUT

FOR KRISTIN,
WORLD-CLASS ASSISTANT

Cover photo courtesy of Bill Hennefrund

Photos courtesy of Red Acre Farm Hearing Dog Center: pp. 3,
17, 19, 20; Bill Hennefrund: pp. 4, 7, 10, 12, 14; Steve Yeager/
Canine Companions for Independence: pp. 23, 24; Support Dogs,
Inc.: p. 25; Lawrence Migdale/Photo Researchers: p. 27.

Library of Congress Cataloging-in-Publication Data

Ring, Elizabeth, 1920-
Assistance dogs: in special service / by Elizabeth Ring.
p.   cm.— (Good Dogs!)
Includes bibliographical references and index.
Summary: Describes the work of dogs that are
specially trained to assist blind, deaf, or disabled people.
ISBN 1-56294-290-5 (lib. bdg.)
1. Service dogs—United States—Juvenile literature.
[1. Working dogs.   2. Dogs.] I. Title. II. Series.
HV1569.6.R56 1993
362.4'0483—DC20   93-735   CIP   AC

Published by The Millbrook Press
2 Old New Milford Road
Brookfield, Connecticut 06804

ASSISTANCE DOGS

Dogs of many breeds play a special role by assisting
blind, deaf, and disabled people.

Early one fine sunny morning, Mary Hook and her dog Nemo were walking along a sidewalk in their hometown of Windsor, Connecticut. It was a route they took often and knew well. The air smelled fresh after a stormy night, and both Mary and Nemo were enjoying their stroll.

Suddenly, Nemo, a German shepherd trained to be a guide dog, stopped short in the middle of a block. Mary, who was blind, started to reach out to find what might lie in their path. But before she had time to investigate, Nemo turned her toward the street. Mary trusted her dog, so she followed Nemo along the curb for a way, and then back to the sidewalk.

"Good boy, Nemo!" Mary said, patting the dog's head—for what reason she did not know.

Imagine how thankful Mary felt when, later, she was told that Nemo had no doubt saved her life. A live wire, torn loose by the previous night's storm, had been dangling right in the middle of the sidewalk, at the very spot where Nemo had steered her toward the street.

"I could have been electrocuted!" Mary realized. She gave Nemo a few extra hugs.

Nemo is one of the thousands of dogs that live among us as helpers and friends. The relationship goes back hundreds of years. No one knows exactly how, when, or why dogs and people first got together. But at some time in the ancient past, wolves and wild dogs became tame enough to share in people's lives— and that has proved to be a good thing for both people and dogs.

How might it have come about that dogs and people connected? Maybe, scientists guess, back when people lived in caves, a hungry wolf came begging for food and stayed to become a dependable hunting companion. Or perhaps a jackal—lost from its wild-dog pack—found friends around a campfire and stayed to become a useful part of a human family.

All we know for sure is that today no other animal—not a horse, cat, cow, or hamster—is so at home with us as a dog. No other animal so enjoys our company or is so willing to please us in every possible way.

Among our dog friends are many helpers, and none help us more than dogs that assist blind, deaf, or disabled people.

GUIDE DOGS · Guide dogs serve as the eyes of blind people. Nemo was a typical guide dog. He went everywhere Mary went. He was beside her bed at night and was right there for her when she got up in the morning. Dressed in his harness (which Mary called his "business suit"), Nemo was accepted in all kinds of public places where most dogs are not welcome. He led her along busy streets, through shopping malls, in and out of buses and cars, and up and down stairs and escalators. He often went with her and her friends to the theater or the ballpark. Because of Nemo's excellent training, Mary could go just about anywhere she wanted.

In their walks around town, Nemo was trained to stop at every curb, waiting for Mary to say "forward" or "right" or "left," or give some other command. Once, when she didn't know the way out of a store, Mary said, "Nemo, find outside." And he led her to the exit door.

But what if Mary had insisted on crossing a street, not aware that a car was coming? Nemo had been taught "intelligent disobedience," and he would refuse to take her into the street until it was safe.

With the help of Nemo, a German shepherd guide dog, Mary Hook, who is blind, can go almost anywhere she wants.

The first training school for guide dogs was established in Germany in 1916 to train German shepherds to lead soldiers blinded in World War I. Thirteen years later, in 1929, German shepherds (brought from Germany) were the first dogs to be trained at the first guide-dog school in the United States. This school, called The Seeing Eye, located in Morristown, New Jersey, has trained many thousands of guide dogs over the years.

Today there are many other American guide-dog training centers, each with its own special program. Nemo was trained at the Fidelco Guide Dog Foundation in Bloomfield, Connecticut. Many schools, like Fidelco, breed the pups they train. Other schools train dogs that are donated, bought from kennels, or found at dog shelters.

All dogs bred or chosen for training must have the qualities needed for guide-dog work: strength, endurance, intelligence, friendliness, and an ability to learn and respond to many different commands. Each dog's temperament (personality) counts, too. Even within one litter, pups differ—just as we differ from our brothers and sisters. Not every dog (even carefully bred ones) can pass all the training-school tests.

Some guide-dog schools train only German shepherds. At other guide-dog schools, German shepherds, golden retrievers, and Labrador retrievers are favored for training. But other breeds make suitable guide dogs, too: collies, weimaraners, Doberman pinschers, Alaskan malamutes, boxers, and many more, including mixed breeds whose parentage is something of a mystery.

It costs thousands of dollars to train a guide dog. However, blind people may obtain a dog for a very small fee, sometimes for free. Funds come from individuals, businesses, foundations, and other groups that want to support the training centers.

Although it takes highly skilled dog trainers to teach guide dogs, volunteers are key to the success of a training center. Unpaid volunteers (all dog lovers, of course) work in kennels, on the grounds, and in offices. They help the trainers, keep records, clean floors, care for newborn pups, and feed, groom, and exercise the dogs. In other words, they do whatever is needed.

In some guide-dog training programs, a puppy's first training may take place at the training center or at the home of a trainer. Most often, however, a pup's first home is with a volunteer foster family. The pup lives with the family from the time it is two or three months old until it is about a year or a year and a half old.

The pup becomes one of the family. At the same time, it learns to be a "good dog." It is taught not to beg for food or make puddles on the floor. It learns to sit, to lie down, to stay, and to greet visitors politely. This training is called "basic obedience."

The dog goes wherever the family goes. It learns its way up and down city streets and along country roads. It rides in cars and on buses. If somebody goes jogging or swimming or even mountain climbing, the dog might tag along. In other words, the dog gets used to all kinds of family activities and learns to adapt

Guide-dog puppies are often raised by volunteers like Mary Anne and
Nelson Hilpert, seen here with Audrey, their ninth foster pup, and
Memphis, a 7-year-old German shepherd who helps mother the pups.

easily to a variety of human ways—and this will help it adapt to a blind partner's life-style.

When the time comes for serious guide-dog training at the training school, it is sometimes hard for the family to give the dog up. But the family has known from the start that it was raising the dog to become an important part of a blind person's life. Many families raise several guide-dog pups. Welcoming a new puppy makes it a bit easier to give up the school-age dog.

The first days at school may be puzzling to a young dog. Where is its family? Where is its rug alongside its best friend's—often a child's—bed? But within a few days the dog's trainer becomes its new best friend. The two are together much of the time, at the kennel and sometimes in the trainer's home. Soon, the dog is having a fine time playing "training games." Training is always made fun. A guide dog has to *like* its work.

During training, the dog gets used to wearing a harness. Attached to the harness is a hard U-shaped handle that the blind person will hold onto. With the harness around its body, the dog is taught to pull forward while walking on the left side and slightly ahead of the trainer.

It usually takes a dog several days to learn to stop at each curb and wait for a command to go forward or turn. But practicing over and over again pays off. Learning to lead a blind person safely around trees, lampposts, parking meters, and other obstacles takes many tries, too.

Guide dog Michi stops at a curb and waits for a command from Fidelco trainer Peter Mowicki. Michi was trained to stay at a curb whenever a car is coming—no matter what command is given.

Before long, most dogs are diving eagerly into their harnesses, loving the work they do so well and enjoying the praise and rewards they receive. In five or six months they are fully trained and ready to meet their working partners.

Nemo met Mary Hook three years after a serious illness left Mary blind at age eighteen. In those three years, she had found life very difficult. She had had to rely on other people to help her get around. Having Nemo as her constant companion gave Mary a freedom she had not known since she had gone blind.

Mary and Nemo were trained to work together at Mary's home. At many guide-dog schools, blind people live at the school for a few weeks while they are learning to work with their dogs. At other schools, like Fidelco, the dog and its trainer go to the blind person's home. That way, while the person is learning how to handle and respond to the dog, the dog is getting used to the home, streets, and neighborhood where its partner lives.

Great care is taken to make sure that a dog and a person are well matched. Mary and Nemo took to each other right away. Then slowly and steadily during the training period, Mary and Nemo "bonded." That is, they formed the special, close friendship that many dogs and their human companions share. Nemo was happy with his new best friend. Mary learned to trust Nemo's guidance. She learned, too, to care for her dog—to feed him, brush him, take him for runs in the park. Within four weeks, they were working and playing together as if they had always

Mary and Nemo were carefully matched and then
trained to work together.

been on their own. After that, for a while, their trainer checked back with them now and then to see how they were getting along.

With Nemo to guide her, Mary was able to live a full life. She worked two days a week at Fidelco, counseling people who wanted guide dogs. She and Nemo visited schools, civic groups, and other places where Mary talked about guide-dog work, and Nemo showed what he could do.

What happens to a guide dog when its working days are over at age ten or twelve? The dog has several opportunities. It may stay with its partner, even though a younger dog becomes the working guide dog. It may go back to its foster-home family, or it may make its home with a new best friend. Even an old guide dog is adaptable.

HEARING DOGS · Betty Smith and her hearing dog, Chico, were used to riding buses together. Betty was a teacher's aide and an administrative assistant in Cambridge, Massachusetts, and she had many interests that meant going here and there often. Ever since Betty had lost her hearing at age thirty-seven, Chico had been her constant companion, at home, at work, and around town.

Chico, a small dog (part Chihuahua), always behaved perfectly on a bus. On his leash on the floor beside Betty, he lay still until it was time to get off. But on one trip, Chico kept pulling on his leash, urging Betty toward the bus door.

Betty was baffled. She and Chico were nowhere near their bus stop. Why was Chico behaving so unlike his usual self? She kept telling him to lie down, and he kept getting up and pawing her, plainly telling her: "Come to the door."

Finally, Betty followed Chico off the bus, just to quiet the dog down. Only when she reached the sidewalk did she discover why Chico had insisted on leaving: The bus roof was on fire. Betty quickly called to the bus driver. Chico had not only helped Betty, he had alerted a whole busful of people.

Chico had been trained to help a deaf person at Red Acre Farm Hearing Dog Center in Stow, Massachusetts. But telling Betty to get off a burning bus was not part of Chico's training. He somehow sensed that something unusual was going on. Some instinct must have told him to get himself and Betty off that bus.

"Good dog, Chico!" Betty said over and over again that day.

Dogs make perfect companions for many deaf people and people who find it hard to hear. Dogs hear much better than people, even people who can hear perfectly well. Dogs hear sounds that people cannot hear at all: sounds in the distance, faint sounds nearby, and very high and low sounds. Most people can hear about 30,000 sound waves each second; a dog hears between 75,000 and 100,000.

Hearing-dog programs were started later than guide-dog programs. The first hearing-dog program was organized by the American Humane Association in Denver, Colorado, in 1976.

Betty Smith and Chico, her hearing dog, are constant companions.

Now there are numerous training centers, such as Red Acre Farm, around the country. Hearing dogs are given free to their deaf or hard-of-hearing partners. Donations alone supply the thousands of dollars it costs to train each hearing dog.

Training for hearing dogs is much the same as for guide dogs. With experienced trainers, dogs practice over and over how to respond to certain signals at certain times. Unlike guide dogs, however, hearing dogs must act without any commands from their partners (who, of course, can't hear the noises that need their attention).

Most hearing dogs come from animal shelters or from people who give their dogs away. Most are mixed breeds: shepherd and spaniel, or poodle and collie, or some other combination.

All dogs chosen for training as hearing dogs are carefully tested. While they do not need to have the size, strength, or endurance needed by guide dogs, they must be healthy, intelligent, friendly, lively and alert, eager to please, and easy to train. Most of all, hearing dogs must be quick to act when they hear certain sounds.

During about four months of training, hearing dogs learn to play the "games" that make them so helpful to deaf people. The dog wakes its partner when an alarm clock rings by pawing or (if it is a small dog) jumping up on the bed. When a bell, buzzer, chime, or knock sounds at the door, the dog paws its partner to get attention. Then it runs to the door and sits down until its partner comes to the door. In the same way, the dog alerts its partner

Hearing dogs are trained to alert their partners to all kinds of sounds—from a ringing telephone to a whistling teapot.

when its partner's name is called, when a teapot whistles, or when a phone rings. (Many phones have special equipment for deaf people, such as a teleprinter that types messages that can be read.)

When the alarm clock rings, small hearing dogs may
wake their partners by jumping on the bed.

All hearing dogs learn to alert their partners when a smoke alarm goes off. But at this particular sound, instead of leading the person to the alarm (which might be close to where a fire has started), the dog is taught to lie down at its partner's feet, blocking the person's path.

Many hearing dogs are trained for special duty, depending on the different needs of deaf people. Some learn to signal when a baby cries or when a child calls. Other dogs, like Chico, are trained to accompany their on-the-go partners to offices, restaurants, stores, and theaters—even on planes, trains, and boats.

When a hearing dog works away from home, it wears a special orange vest or leash that tells the public (as a guide dog's harness does) that this is a dog doing an important job. The partner also carries an identification card that explains the dog's presence in places where most dogs are not usually allowed.

Some hearing dogs are extra alert and signal when they hear any unusual sound. One dog insisted that its partner check out a banging shutter. Another led its partner to a dripping faucet in a basement. Betty Smith's dog, Chico, was certainly extra alert that day on the burning bus!

SERVICE DOGS · The day Brad Gabrielson, of Jamestown, North Dakota, tumbled out of his wheelchair, his service dog, Bo, knew just what to do: He pulled on a string that was tied to a lever by the front door. The door opened and Bo bounded down the street, going from house to house, barking at doors. Finally, at one house, someone answered his call. Bo took the neighbor's fingers lightly in his mouth and led him straight home to Brad.

Brad suffers from cerebral palsy, a disability that makes it difficult for him to control his muscles. When he fell, the wheelchair fell on top of him. Since nobody else was at home, he could have been trapped there all day—except for Bo's intelligence and his trained response in fetching Brad's neighbor.

"Good boy, Bo," both Brad and his neighbor said to the dog.

Bo is a gentle, good-natured golden retriever. Golden retrievers and Labrador retrievers are greatly favored for service-dog work. Besides being friendly dogs, retrievers are very good at retrieving—as Bo showed by bringing the neighbor to Brad. Dozens of times a day, a service dog may be called upon to fetch things to its partner—a magazine from a table, perhaps, or a coin that has dropped to the floor.

The first training center for service dogs, called Canine Companions for Independence (CCI), was started in 1975 in Santa Rosa, California. Today CCI has branches in New York, Florida, and Ohio. Several other organizations have established service-dog training centers across the United States.

The training for a service dog is quite special. It takes about eight months, instead of the five or six months it takes to train a guide dog or hearing dog. A CCI service dog learns up to sixty separate commands. When the dogs are through school, many can help even severely disabled people such as Brad Gabrielson.

Service dogs can do some amazing things. They learn to pick things up very carefully—sometimes by practicing with

Jennifer Holland and her service dog Gimli, a golden retriever, are graduates of training programs at Canine Companions for Independence (CCI).

eggs. With that skill and the intelligence to string together a number of different simple commands (such as "look," "up," and "get it"), a trained dog can carefully pluck an item from a supermarket or library shelf.

Service dog
Drake opens
a door for his
partner, Gene
Hopkins.

Service dogs are taught to turn light switches on and off, press elevator buttons, help their owners on and off buses, and carry bags. A service dog can also lift and lower window shades, open and shut doors and drawers, lock and unlock wheelchairs, and pull them along sidewalks and across streets.

Many service dogs are taught to "take the phone." At the command, they pick up a cordless telephone by a special handle and carry it to their partner—to answer or make a call.

Service dog Alex and his partner, Phyllis Burdge, demonstrate a wheelchair pull.

There are many stories of dogs like Bo that give extraordinary help to their owners. One little boy in Florida started to fall out of his wheelchair on a school bus. His dog quickly placed himself against the boy's chest and eased his body to the floor, breaking his fall. Another person's electric wheelchair lost power in the middle of a street. Her dog pulled the chair to the curb.

A few *very* special dogs help people who suffer from epilepsy, a disease that causes seizures that often make the people lose consciousness. Some dogs are able to detect when a seizure is coming on. The dogs try to get their partners safely to a bed or chair. Failing that, they alert someone else to come help. So far, no one knows exactly how the dogs know an attack is coming on even before the person does. Could it be that the dog senses a change in the person's perspiration or rate of breathing? Or is there something else that signals to the dog that something is not right? Studies are being made.

The assistance, companionship, comfort, and joy all service dogs give their partners are impossible for the partners to measure.

Phyllis Burdge, whose dog Alex was trained at Support Dogs, Inc., in St. Louis, Missouri, had muscular dystrophy. She depended on Alex for daily care. Even when she had to go into the hospital for treatments, Alex—with special permission—always went with her. One of those times, when he was alone in Phyllis's room with her, her heart slowed down and she almost stopped breathing. Alex sensed that something was wrong and pulled the call-light cord to get help from the nurses.

A service dog in training learns to accompany people anywhere.

Phyllis once said: "My dog may never have dragged me from a burning building or saved me from drowning, but he saves my life every day. Without him I could not live my life to its fullest, doing all I can do and being all I can be."

Can you imagine any assistance dog's partner who would not agree? Some dogs and some people simply need each other.

FURTHER READING

Arnold, Caroline. *A Guide Dog Puppy Grows Up*. Orlando: Harcourt Brace Jovanovich, 1991.

Curtis, Patricia. *Cindy, a Hearing Ear Dog*. New York: Dutton, 1981.

Emert, Phyllis R. *Guide Dogs*. New York: Crestwood, 1985.

————. *Hearing-Ear Dogs*. New York: Crestwood, 1985.

Yates, Elizabeth. *Sound Friendships: The Story of Willa and her Hearing Ear Dog*. Woodstock, Vt.: The Countryman Press, 1987.

INDEX

ABOUT THE AUTHOR

Free-lance writer and editor Elizabeth Ring is a former teacher and an editor at *Ranger Rick's Nature Magazine*. Her previous books for children include two biographies, *Rachel Carson: Caring for the Earth* and *Henry David Thoreau: In Step With Nature*, published by The Millbrook Press. She has also written a range of programs on environmental subjects for the National Wildlife Federation. She lives in Woodbury, Connecticut, with her husband, writer and photographer William Hennefrund. Although five dogs have been a part of the family over the years, three cats are their current companions.